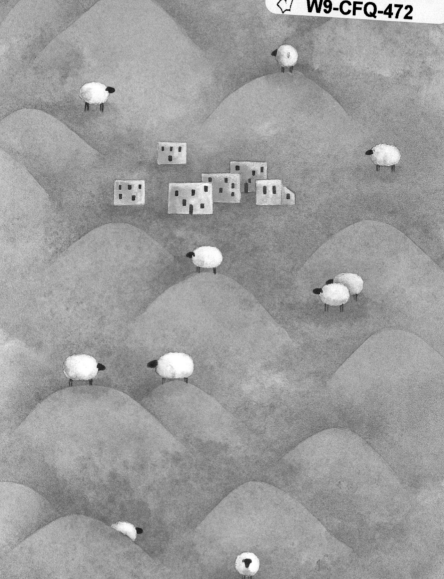

The First Christmas

Enid Blyton

It's wonderful to see that Enid Blyton's inspirational writing is being made available to today's young readers.

Her writing style has the same richness of language that can be found in the King James version of the Bible, so new readers will be treated to not only good stories but her "poetry in voice" as well.

Tomie dePaola

The FIRST Christmas

Enid Blyton

Illustrated by Rosalind Hudson

ELEMENT
CHILDREN'S BOOKS

SHAFTESBURY, DORSET · BOSTON, MASSACHUSETTS · MELBOURNE, VICTORIA

Enid Blyton

Text © Enid Blyton Limited 1945
All Rights Reserved

Enid Blyton's signature is a trademark of Enid Blyton Limited
For further information please contact www.blyton.com

First published in Great Britain by Methuen in 1945
First published by Element Children's Books in 1998,
Shaftesbury, Dorset SP7 8BP
Published in the USA in 1998 by Element Books Inc.
160 North Washington Street, Boston MA 02114

Published in Australia in 1998 by Element Books Limited
and distributed by Penguin Books Australia Ltd,
487 Maroondah Highway, Ringwood, Victoria 3134

British Library Cataloguing in Publication data available.

Library of Congress Cataloging in Publication data available.

ISBN 1 901881 32 6

Cover design by Gabrielle Morton

Cover and endpapers © 1998 Diana Mayo

Inside illustrations © 1998 Rosalind Hudson

Typeset by Dorchester Typesetting Group Ltd
Printed and bound in Great Britain by Creative Print and Design

The First Christmas

A long, long time ago, there lived a little girl called Mary. Her home was in the village of Nazareth, and she lived with her father and mother.

Sometimes Mary heard her parents talking sadly about their country.

"The Romans rule over us now," said her father. "Our greatness is gone. Our country belongs to Rome. But we must not forget what the Lord God promised us many years ago."

"What did he promise?" asked Mary. "Did he promise to make us a great people again?"

"Yes," said her father. "He promised he would send us a king, who would save us and would be the greatest king the world has ever known."

"Will the king come soon?" asked Mary. "I want to see him. Is he born yet?"

"No one knows when the great king will come," said her father.

Mary thought a great deal about the wonderful king as she grew up. She wished she were a royal princess, and then perhaps she might have had the honor of being his mother. But she was only a little peasant girl.

Mary grew up into a good and thoughtful girl. And then one day something beautiful happened to her.

An angel came to her. First there shone a brilliant light, so that Mary was almost dazzled.

Then she saw, in the middle of the light, a beautiful angel, who looked at her with love and kindness.

Mary gazed at the angel half afraid of such a wonderful being. His wings shone behind him, and he spoke in a clear and joyful voice. He told Mary something so surprising that she could hardly believe it was true.

"Hail, Mary!" said the angel. "I bring you great news. You are to have a little son, and you shall call him Jesus. He shall be great, and shall be called the Son of the Highest. Of his kingdom there shall be no end."

Mary was full of wonder. Could it be true that the great savior was to come to her?

"But how can this thing be?" said Mary, trembling with joy and fear.

"The baby shall be the son of God," said the angel. "He shall be a holy child, and he shall reign over his people, and shall be the greatest king that has ever lived."

Mary was full of joy to hear such wonderful news. She, a little village girl, was to have the holy baby, the son of God. No princess had been chosen for his mother; Mary was to have him and love him, and watch over his babyhood and childhood.

The angel stood before her, gazing at her with his shining eyes. Mary knew she must answer. She spoke to him humbly but proudly.

"Behold the handmaid of the Lord. I am ready to do whatever he wishes."

The bright light faded and with it went the beautiful angel. Mary was alone again. She sat thinking of all that the angel had said.

"I am to have the little son of God. He will be my own baby. I shall hold him in my arms and sing to him," she thought. "And one day he will be a great king. But how can that be, for I, his mother, am only a peasant girl?"

In Mary's village there was a carpenter called Joseph. He loved Mary, for she was sweet and gentle. He asked her to be his wife, and that made Mary happy. She knew she would like to go and live with Joseph in his little white house.

One night an angel came to Joseph too, and told him Mary's great secret.

"God has promised that he will send the baby king to Mary," said the angel. "His name shall be Jesus, and he shall be great."

Joseph bowed himself down before the beautiful angel, and listened in wonder. When the angel had gone, Joseph went to Mary and told her that he knew her wonderful secret.

"Now we shall be able to welcome the little king together," said Mary, joyfully. "Oh, Joseph, it will be wonderful to have such a holy child, the son of God, whose kingdom shall have no end."

Mary and Joseph were very happy in their little white house on the hillside. Mary did the work in the house, and got ready the meals. She went to fetch water from the well.

Sometimes she went to sit with Joseph as he did his carpentry. She knew all his shining tools and liked to see him use them.

He liked her to be there with him, too, for he loved his gentle, kindly wife. He showed her all the things he made. She was proud when people came to buy his work and praised what he had done.

The summer went by in happiness. The autumn came, and Mary thought longingly of the little baby who would soon come to her.

"I am only the wife of a village carpenter," thought Mary, "and yet I am to have a little prince for my own, the baby king, the son of God. He will not be born in a palace. He will not have servants to look after him. He will have only me, but I shall love him with all my heart."

And so she and Joseph waited patiently for the baby son of God to come. Soon it would be time for him to be born.

One day, when the autumn had gone and winter had come, strange men came to Mary's village, and to all the towns round about.

They carried with them big notices, which they put up everywhere. The people went to read them, and the children tried to read them too.

The people read the notices with sad faces.

The children pulled at their arms. "Tell us what the notices say. What must we do? Is it a command from the Roman emperor, who rules over us?"

"Yes," said their parents, unhappily. "The emperor wants money. He has commanded that all of us shall pay him money – a tax, it is called. How can we afford it?"

"We shall have to pay," said the chief men of the village. "The Romans are powerful. They will send their soldiers into our villages, and kill us if we do not pay."

"Where must we pay?" asked the people. "Who will take the money?"

"The notice says that every one of us must go to our own town, and there we must give our names and pay the money," said the chief men.

Now many of the people had left their home-towns, and had gone to live in other places. They looked at one another in dismay.

"It is bad enough to have to pay a tax, but it is a shame to make us travel so far in winter," said many of the men. "Some of us must go a whole day's journey and more to get to our home-towns!"

"We must do it," said the chief men. "The Romans have conquered us. They are our rulers, and we must obey. Each of us must pay the tax in his home-town, no matter how far away it is."

Joseph went to tell Mary the news. She was sad.

"Oh, Joseph," she said, "I am not very strong just now. I do not want to travel. Can we not pay the tax here in Nazareth?"

"Nazareth is not our home-town," said Joseph, and he was sad too, for he did not want to travel in the wintertime, when Mary did not feel strong. "We must go to Bethlehem, up in the hills, because we both belong to the family of David, and that is our town, the little city of Bethlehem. We must go there to pay our tax."

"I cannot walk so far," said Mary. "It is a long, long way away. I shall be so tired, Joseph."

"You shall ride on our little donkey," said Joseph. "Do not be afraid, Mary. I will look after you. The donkey will carry you well, and I shall walk beside you."

"When must we go?" asked Mary.

"As soon as we can," said Joseph, "because we have not much time to pay the tax. We must start tomorrow."

All that day Mary was very busy. She cleared up the house. She packed things to take with her. She put food into a basket for herself and Joseph. Joseph too was busy. He tidied his workshop, and put away his tools.

The next day everything was ready for them to start. Joseph fetched the little donkey and saddled him.

He lifted Mary gently on to his back. "Now we are ready," he said, and he shut the door of the little white house. "Let us go. We will go slowly, then you will not get too tired, Mary."

They set off down the hillside. If Mary had felt stronger she would have enjoyed the long ride through the hills. The little donkey walked along steadily, and Joseph strode beside him.

They were not the only ones who took the

road to Bethlehem. Many others were going there too, for all who belonged to the family of David had to go to the same place, to give in their names and pay the tax.

Some of their friends went along the same road. They spoke to Joseph.

"It is such a long way to Bethlehem. What a pity that Mary has to go just when she is not feeling strong! It is a good thing you have a sturdy little donkey."

Other people went faster than they did, but Joseph would not hurry the donkey. Patiently he walked beside Mary, talking to her, and trying to lead the donkey over the best and smoothest paths.

But before they came to the end of the journey Mary was very tired. She drooped over the donkey, and Joseph was sad to see her pale face.

"Are we nearly there, Joseph?" asked Mary. "I cannot go much further."

Joseph put his hand on the donkey and stopped him for a moment. "Look, Mary," he said, pointing up the hillside, "can you see that little town up there on the hill? That is

Bethlehem. See, we shall pass by these fields where the shepherds watch their sheep – and take that path beyond – and soon we shall be at the gates of Bethlehem."

Mary looked at the little town on the hill. It still seemed a great distance away.

"It will be night-time before we get there, Joseph," she said. "I am so tired."

"I will take you to an inn," said Joseph. "I will find you a quiet room, Mary, where you can lie down and rest. I will make you a fire to warm yourself by. How cold your hands are, and how tired you look! It will not be long now before you are resting at the inn."

Mary smiled down at kind Joseph. He had to walk while she rode. But soon they would both be able to rest.

The road up to Bethlehem was very steep.

It wound up the hillside, and night fell as they came to the top.

"See how the lights of Bethlehem twinkle," said Joseph. "We shall soon be out of this cold wind, Mary, and you will find a welcome at the inn. The donkey too is tired, and will be glad of a stable to rest in."

They came into the town. It was very, very full of people. Mary spoke to Joseph anxiously.

"Joseph, I feel so tired and ill. Take me to the inn quickly."

Joseph guided the donkey to a wayside inn. Lights shone from the window, and cheerful voices talked together. Joseph called loudly for the innkeeper.

He came to the doorway. "Have you room for us?" asked Joseph. "My wife is not well and she is very tired, for we have come a long way."

"Sir, my inn is full," said the man. "I have no bed for you, and there is nowhere in the town that has a sleeping-place tonight. The city is full of people."

"No room for us," said Joseph, in despair. "Then what shall we do? See my poor wife, how tired and ill she looks."

"I am sorry," said the innkeeper. "If I had a bed I would give it to you. But there is no place for you here."

He looked at Mary, sitting so patiently on

the donkey. He saw her white face, and big, tired eyes, and he was sad for her. He rubbed his chin and wondered what to do, for he was a kindly man.

J ust as Joseph was turning away with the donkey, the innkeeper spoke again.

"Wait," he said. "I have a cave at the back of my inn, a stable, where the oxen sleep. You can rest there for the night, if you wish. That

is the only place I have to offer you."

Joseph looked at Mary, and she nodded her head. "Yes, Joseph," she said, "I will go there and rest. I cannot go any further tonight."

"I will send a servant to sweep out the stable," said the innkeeper. "He can put down fresh straw. The animals will be around you all night, and you will smell their warm bodies. But it is the only place I have for you."

"We will go there," said Joseph. So the innkeeper called a servant, and he took Mary and Joseph to the stable at the back of the inn. Then the servant took a broom and swept the floor. He put down fresh, clean straw for Mary to lie on.

Joseph lifted her tenderly off the tired donkey. She sank down into the straw, and lay there thankfully, glad to be out of the cold wind, and resting at last.

The donkey too was glad to be free of his heavy burden. He munched his hay gladly, standing near to Mary, for even the stable was full of animals belonging to the innkeeper and to the other travelers. Mary saw their warm breath rising up by the light of the lantern that the servant had put in the stable.

The straw seemed a soft and welcome bed to Mary. Joseph looked after her tenderly. He gave her milk to drink, and he folded a rug to make her a pillow for her head. The wind came in at the open doorway of the stable, and Joseph saw that Mary felt it.

So he took off his cloak and hung it carefully across the doorway to keep out the wind. Mary smiled up at him, but he saw that she was in pain, and her face was very white.

"Soon you will be warm and rested," he said to Mary. "It is a strange place to sleep in, but it is the best we could find."

"Joseph, the little son of God will be born here tonight," said Mary. "Soon I shall hold him in my arms."

What a peculiar place for a little baby to come to! The oxen stamped as they stood in their stalls, and the little donkey stood looking down at Mary as he munched his supper. The lantern shone and flickered over the dark stable.

And that night, in the stable, the little son of God was born. The baby king was there, in Mary's arms, and her lips were against his soft cheek.

"See, Joseph – the son of God is born!" said

Mary. "He is here at last. How beautiful he is!"

Joseph knelt down in the straw beside Mary and looked in awe and wonder at the tiny child. He remembered what the angel had said to him and to Mary. This was indeed the little son of God, the king of the whole world, come to them just as the angel had said.

Mary took the baby on her knee and wondered what to do with him. There was no cradle, no bed. There was no other woman to help her with the little child. She must do everything herself.

"What tiny nails he has – and how silky his skin is," thought Mary, as she tended the baby lovingly. "The hair on his head is like down. Surely there never was a child like this before!"

"Joseph, I must wrap the baby in his swaddling-clothes," said Mary, at last. "I brought them with me. Will you get them for me?"

Joseph found the roll of linen cloth that Mary had made for her baby. She had carefully packed it to bring with her. Joseph unrolled it for her.

Swaddling-clothes were the first clothes a baby wore in those far-off days. Mothers wrapped the linen cloth round and round their babies, so that the little things felt safe and cozy.

Mary took the linen cloth that Joseph held out to her, and began to twist it round the tiny child. She sang softly to him as she put on his swaddling-clothes. She was very happy.

"See how good he is!" she said to Joseph. "He does not cry at all. There, my little lamb, you are ready to sleep."

She sat with him on her knee for a little while, but Joseph could see that she was very tired. She needed to go to sleep too. She could not sit up all night holding the baby on her knee.

"You must sleep, Mary," said Joseph.

"But where shall I put the little one if I lie down to sleep?" said Mary. "I cannot put him down on this rough straw. He needs a soft bed. We have no cradle for him, this little son of God."

J oseph looked all round the stable. He saw the mangers there, that the animals ate from. Some were fixed to the wall, others, made of wood, were placed here and there on the ground, ready to be taken to any animal needing food.

"Mary, we will put him in a manger," said Joseph. "He is small enough to go in, and he will be safe and cozy there. I can put some hay inside the manger and that will make him a soft bed."

"Yes, he shall have a manger for a bed," said Mary. "Look, Joseph, you can take some of our donkey's hay – he will not mind."

So Joseph pulled away some of the little donkey's hay, and put it into the manger. It made a very soft, sweet-smelling bed for the little Jesus.

Mary laid the baby down gently. She covered him with a little rug. He looked round, sleepily, not knowing what he saw, for he was so new and small. Then he shut his eyes.

"He is asleep!" said Mary, and she went to lie down in the straw again. She was very tired. She put her head on the rolled-up rug, and looked up at Joseph. She smiled at him.

"Now we will all sleep," she said. "You too, poor, tired Joseph. The oxen will sleep as they stand in their stalls, the little donkey will sleep, and the doves that have cooed on the rafters above will sleep again too."

Mary slept, and Jesus slept too, in his manger of hay. But Joseph did not sleep. He guarded Mary and Jesus all night long.

That was the very first Christmas, when Jesus Christ, the little son of God, was born. But no one knew except Mary and Joseph. No bells rang out to tell the world that he was born. Everyone in Bethlehem slept, and not one man or woman knew that there was a holy baby in the stable at the back of the inn.

But the angels in heaven knew that the son of God was born. They had been keeping watch over Bethlehem, and they knew that the baby in the stable was to be the greatest king in the world.

Their hearts were full of joy. They sang glad songs to one another as they watched over the city. "A savior is born this day! What tidings of joy! The son of God is born in the city of David!"

They wanted to tell someone, but there was no one to tell. Everyone in the city was fast asleep. Not one person seemed to be awake to hear the wonderful news.

The angels wanted to come into our world to spread the joyful news. Everyone must know! They looked round for any who might be awake.

But the only people awake that night were the shepherds on the hillside outside Bethlehem. Always some of them kept awake at night to guard their sheep.

Sometimes fierce wolves came seeking for lambs to carry away at night. Then the shepherds would drive them away, and bring the lambs nearer their fire.

The wolves did not like the gleaming flames of the fire.

The shepherds took it in turn to guard their

sheep at night. In wintertime it was cold up on the hill, and they wrapped their thick clothes warmly round them, and crouched over their fire.

Around them lay the sheep with their little lambs.

No lamb wandered away from its mother at night unless it was very foolish. Sometimes the sheep saw the gleam of fierce green eyes in the distance, and they baaed to their lambs

to come closer, closer, for the wolf was near.

That night the shepherds sat as usual round their fire. They were sleepy and tired, but it was their turn to guard the sheep, so they must keep awake.

"Let us talk," said one big shepherd. "My eyes will stay open if we talk. How cold the wind is tonight."

"Let us talk of all the people we have seen going up the road to the town of Bethlehem," said another shepherd.

"Never in my life have I seen so many

people," said a third shepherd, and he held his hands over the fire to warm them. "How can they all find room to sleep there?"

"Every inn is full," said the fourth shepherd. "There is no place left for any late traveler."

"There must be a great deal of money in Bethlehem tonight," said the first shepherd. "You know that all these travelers have come to pay money to the Roman emperor."

"Yes – he takes as much money from us as he can," said another shepherd. "But wait – God has promised to send us a savior one day – a great king to rule over us."

"If only this king would come in our lifetime!" said the first shepherd. "I should like to bow myself down before a king as great as that."

So they talked to one another in the darkness of the night, never dreaming that the king, the great savior, was even then lying in the stable of the inn.

A lamb came nearer to them, and their dog raised his head. Then, seeing that it was only one of the lambs, he put his head down on his paws again.

But he was uneasy. He raised his head again after a minute or two, and growled a little. One of the shepherds stroked his soft head.

"What is it, old dog? Do you smell a wolf? What is the matter with you?"

The shepherds looked all around, but they could see and hear nothing unusual. Their sheep were quiet. There was no dark wolf-shadow creeping around.

But then something strange began to happen. The angels had decided that they would tell the wakeful shepherds on the hillside their wonderful news. They were coming to tell them!

And suddenly, over that dark hillside, a great light appeared in the sky. The dog rose to his feet and trembled. The shepherds looked up in wonder. What was this brilliance?

The light grew brighter, and the shepherds were dazzled when they looked into it. Then the light spread down from the sky, and

rested on the hillside too. It was brighter than day.

The shepherds were afraid. They drew close to one another, and looked round in wonder. What could be happening? Never before had they seen a light like this shining in the middle of the night.

Then, in the midst of the light, a bright being came, an angel with outstretched wings. He was quite near to the shepherds, shining even more brightly than the strange light.

The shepherds were amazed.

"See!" whispered one, catching at the arm of the man next to him. "See – an angel!"

"Yes, surely it is an angel!" said the rest, and they fell upon their knees in fear and wonder.

Some covered their faces, for they were afraid of what they might see next.

Then the angel spoke, and his voice was like purest music.

"Fear not," said the angel, "for behold, I bring you good tidings of great joy, which shall be to all people. For unto you is born this day in the city of David a savior, which is Christ the Lord. And this shall be a sign unto you – you shall find the babe wrapped in swaddling-clothes and lying in a manger."

The shepherds listened in the greatest amazement. The savior born – the promised king! How could this be?

They gazed at the bright and joyful angel, and they knew that he spoke great words. The king was somewhere not far from them, in Bethlehem, the city of David. Somewhere he lay, there in the town, a babe wrapped in swaddling-clothes – and lying in a *manger*!

Then, as they gazed in awe at the angel, another wonderful thing happened. The darkness of the sky above them gave way, and all above and around them appeared a shining host of angels, singing and rejoicing together.

"Glory to God in the highest, and on earth peace, goodwill toward men! Glory to God in the highest, and on earth peace, goodwill toward men!" sang the angels in their bright, clear voices.

The shepherds listened in the utmost wonder. They looked at the sky, so full of angels; they heard the singing and thought it was the most beautiful music they had ever heard.

The song went on and on. "Glory to God in the highest!" The host of angels sang joyfully, and the sky shone with a dazzling light.

And then slowly the brilliance faded. As it faded the darkness came again, and the shining angels were gone. Only the echoes of their song could be heard, faint and far away.

The stars could be seen again. The hillside was as quiet and as dark as it had been before the angels came.

The shepherds looked and listened for a little while longer. They dared not say a word to one another. Perhaps another wonder might happen. They waited, trembling and full of excitement.

But nothing more happened. The sheep stirred in the field around. The dog, who had been very much afraid, crept up to his master

and pressed against him. The man put out his hand and stroked his head.

Then a shepherd spoke in a low and wondering voice.

"Those were angels out of heaven! Is this a dream?"

"No," said another. "It was no dream. But it was a very wonderful thing. What an honor for lowly shepherds like us to see angels!"

"Why did they come to us? What did that first shining angel say?"

Another shepherd spoke in answer. He raised his voice in excitement. "The angel said that the savior had come – the promised king! He said that he was born this night in the city of David! That's Bethlehem, the town up yonder."

"A baby king – born tonight in Bethlehem! We must go and find him!"

"But it's the middle of the night! And besides we don't know where he is."

"The angel said he was in a manger. That means he is in a stable. The inn has a stable. We will go there and see if the baby king is in a manger. He must belong to one of the travelers. Come, let us go quickly!"

The shepherds were so happy and excited at the wonderful news the angels brought, that they felt they must set off at once.

They left their dogs to guard the sheep, except one who went with them. They wrapped their cloaks warmly around them, for the wind on the hillside was cold.

"I shall take the little king one of my new-born lambs," said one shepherd, and he picked up a tiny lamb nearby and carried it in his arms.

They set off over the hillside. They talked as they went, reminding one another of the glorious sight they had seen.

"Hundreds of angels – all shining, with their voices filling the sky!" they said. "We are honored men. The angels came to *us*, and not to the people of Bethlehem!"

They came to the road that led up to the hill-city. The dog pattered at their heels. The little lamb in the shepherd's arms bleated, and he wrapped his cloak around it.

"Maybe an angel will come to show us the way," said a shepherd, looking into the sky. But no angel came. The night-sky was empty and silent now.

Soon they came into the town. They looked for the inn they knew. There it was, a great dark shape in the night.

"Now, what shall we do?" whispered the shepherds. "If we knock on the door, we shall wake everyone, and maybe the innkeeper will be angry with us."

"Still, we must ask him if he has anyone in the stable," said one.

"Let us go and see for ourselves," said another. "We know the way. The stable is at the back of the inn."

They made their way quietly round to the back of the inn.

"Look – there is a light shining out from the stable!" whispered a shepherd. "Do you see it? Someone is there."

Trembling with excitement, the shepherds went to where the light shone out. Was the little king there? Would they find a baby in a manger, wrapped in swaddling-clothes, as the angels had said?

Across the stable doorway hung Joseph's cloak to keep out the wind. The shepherds lifted a corner and peeped into the stable.

A lantern inside lit up the low-roofed, shadowy stable. Oxen were there, standing in their stalls. A little donkey turned his head towards them, wondering who they were.

But the shepherds saw neither oxen nor donkey.

They gazed in wonder at a small, sleeping baby, tucked in a manger. They could see that he was in swaddling-clothes, just as the angel had said.

"See! The baby is there!" whispered one of the shepherds in a trembling voice. "It was no dream we had. It was all real, and the angels brought us true tidings of great joy."

Mary was asleep on the straw. Joseph sat nearby, looking lovingly down at Mary. It was

a sight that the shepherds remembered all
their lives long.

Mary awoke. She heard the whispering
voices. "Someone is outside," she said to
Joseph. "Who can it be?"

Joseph put aside the cloak at the doorway
and saw the shepherds and their dog. He
looked at them in surprise.

"We have come to worship the little king,"
said the shepherds, and they came into the

stable. "The angels told us about him. They told us he was in a manger, wrapped in swaddling-clothes. So we came to find him."

Mary listened in wonder. So angels had come out of heaven to tell of the coming of the holy child! She lifted the baby from his strange cradle, and put him on her knee. The shepherds knelt to worship him.

"He is to be the savior," they whispered to Mary. "The great shining angel told us so. You are the mother of the greatest king in the world."

Mary marveled at the coming of the rough shepherds. She marveled at their tale of the sky shining with singing angels. She listened in wonder when they told her the song the angels sang.

Soon the shepherds went, for Mary was still very tired. One of them left the little lamb with Joseph. It was the baby's first present.

Peace and quietness came again into the stable. The doves in the roof cooed softly and went to sleep again. The oxen turned away their heads, and the donkey slept. Mary slept too, and the holy child lay at rest in his manger. Only Joseph stayed awake, thinking of the tale the shepherds told.

Down the hill went the shepherds, telling one another over and over again of the wonders of that night.

"First the shining angel came, then the sky was full of them," they said. "Then we went to find the little savior, and we saw him in the manger. What fortunate men we are! What a tale we shall have to tell tomorrow! Now – let us be sure we know the words the angels said, for we must teach them to others."

Next day the shepherds told all their friends the wonderful happenings of the night. People marveled to hear their tale.

"Angels came to this field," the children whispered to one another. "Oh, if only we had been awake last night!"

They went to peep at the little baby in the

manger. They gazed at him with love. Here was the baby that angels had sung about. How sweet he was! How they longed to touch his soft cheek and feel his fingers round theirs.

Mary soon grew used to the wondering eyes of the peeping children. She thought of everything that had happened, and she knew that this small child of hers would grow up to be a

great and good man, the finest the world had ever seen.

Soon Bethlehem was empty of travelers, and Joseph took Mary to a house where she might be more comfortable. But Mary did not forget the stable at the back of the inn.

"That was where you were born," she sometimes whispered to the little Jesus. "You came to a stable and slept in a manger – but angels sang at your birth."

Now, about this time there lived some wise and learnèd men in a country to the east. These men watched the stars at night, and studied them, for they said the stars told them many things.

They said that when a new star appeared it meant that something great had happened in the world.

One night a new star swam into the sky. As the night went on, it grew brighter and brighter, until at last it shone so brilliantly that no other stars could be seen.

"This is a wonderful star," said the wise men. "What can it mean? We must look in our old, old books, and see if the new star has come to tell us of some great happening in the world."

They read in their books, and they soon knew what the star meant.

"It means that a great and mighty king is born," they said to one another. "We must follow this star and find the wonderful king. We will take him presents, and worship him."

So they called their servants and told them to get everything ready for a long journey.

"Get our camels ready," they commanded. "Pack food for the journey, and take tents in which to sleep at night, for we must travel a long, long way."

Their servants made haste to get everything ready.

They were excited because they too were to go on this journey, and to follow the star and see where it rested. The wise men had many servants, for in their own land they were kings.

"We will take rich gifts, the best we have, gifts fit for a king," said the wise men, and these were carefully packed too.

Then at last they set off on their swift-footed camels. They had to pass through sandy deserts, but the camels went quickly over the sand, their curious, spreading feet finding sure foothold.

Night after night the great star shone in the
sky, its brilliance filling the world. To the west
went the wise men and their train of servants,

always following the shining star, which
seemed to guide them on their way.

The star led them to the land of the Jews. When they came into that land they went to Jerusalem, where the Jewish kings lived.

"The new-born king will surely be in Jerusalem, in the great palace there," said the wise men to one another. They did not know that the baby Jesus was born in a stable in Bethlehem. All they knew was that a great king had been born, and they felt certain they would find him at the royal palace.

Now in the palace was the king of the Jews, a wicked man called Herod. The Romans allowed him to be king, but he was always frightened in case they might take away his crown. If he feared or hated anyone he had them killed at once.

His servants came to tell him that rich and powerful strangers were at the gates of the palace.

"They have magnificent robes, and ride fine camels," his servants told Herod. "They have many servants and they have traveled a long way. Shall we bring them before you, O King?"

Herod bade them bring the strangers before him. Soon the wise men and their servants came to Herod, and bowed to him. The king looked at them with great curiosity, for they were noble-looking men, with wisdom in their faces.

"Why do you travel here, so far from your own land?" asked Herod, lying in state on his royal couch. Their answer filled his wicked mind with fear.

"Sir, we come to find him that is born King of the Jews," answered the wise men. "We have seen his star in the east, and have come to worship him."

Herod was angry. "I am the King of the Jews," he said. "There is no new-born king here. What is this star you have seen?"

The wise men told the king how they had followed the brilliant star. "But the star cannot mean you, O King," they said. "It means a king new born, one who will be greater than any you have known before."

Then Herod was full of fury and fear. Where could this new-born king be? He would not allow any baby to grow up into a great king. He would kill him!

"I must not let these wise men know that I shall kill this baby," he thought. "I must answer them kindly. I must pretend to help them. And I will tell them to come back to me when they have found the baby, to tell me where he is, so that I too may go and worship him – but I shall kill him!"

Herod did not tell his wicked thoughts to the wise men. Instead he called his learnèd men and bade them read in old books to try to find out where this new-born king would be.

They found out what he wanted to know.

"Our old books tell us that this king will be born in Bethlehem," they said.

"Where is that?" asked the wise men.

"Not far away," said Herod. "It is on a hill not far from Jerusalem. Go there and see if the new king is there. But come back to me and tell me if you find him, for I too will go and kneel before him in worship."

"We will come back," said the wise men, and they turned to go. "We will go now, for we have gifts to lay before this new-born king, and we are eager to see him and worship him."

They went out of the palace, their servants with them. They mounted their camels, and set off on the road to Bethlehem. They had to go down the hill of Jerusalem, and then up another to Bethlehem.

It was evening as they set out to go to Bethlehem. The sun was sinking. It flashed on the jewels the wise men wore; it glinted on their jingling harnesses. Everyone stared as they went by, for it was plain that they were great and powerful men, riding their swift camels.

Then the brilliant star rose and shone out once more.

How it shone that night! It seemed to stand right over the little hillside town of Bethlehem.

"See," said the wise men, "the star is showing us where the new-born king lies. It stands right over Bethlehem!"

Up the quiet hillside they went, the way that Mary and Joseph had taken a little while before. The shepherds were in the fields, watching their sheep as they always did. They heard the jingling harnesses, and stared in astonishment as the grand strangers went by on their striding camels.

The wise men went into the city of Bethlehem. They stopped a woman of the town, and asked her a question.

"Is there a new-born baby here?"

The woman gazed up, half afraid, at the mysterious strangers. "Yes," she said. "There is one in that house yonder. He is there with his mother."

"The star stands right over the house," said the wise men, and they went to it.

They were soon inside, and Mary looked in

wonder and surprise at the three strange visitors. She was even more surprised when they knelt down before her and the little child on her knee, and worshiped him.

"Here is the king we have come to find," said one of the wise men. "Now let us lay our gifts before him."

They had brought royal presents to little Jesus, gifts that were only given to great kings. The servants undid the gifts, and the wise men laid them at the feet of Mary and the child.

"I have brought gold," said one wise man.

"I have brought frankincense," said another.

"And I bring myrrh," said the third. The beautiful jewels, the sweet-smelling scents and the precious spices were there before Mary's wondering eyes. She was full of amazement as she held the little Jesus close

against her.

What sort of child was this, at whose birth angels sang, whom shepherds came to worship, and at whose feet rich kings laid gifts

so rare? Mary looked down at the little head on her breast, and knew that this child belonged not only to her, but to the whole world also.

When they had given the little child their gifts, and had gazed on him to their hearts' content, the wise men said farewell and left.

They left behind them the royal gifts, and Mary marveled at them. Joseph too gazed in wonder at the rich gifts, so rare and precious.

The wise men did not go back to Jerusalem that night, for it was getting late.

"We will stay for the night at the inn," they said, and they went to the very inn where the baby Jesus had been born. Their camels were put in the stable, and the wise men had the best rooms in the inn for themselves.

They were tired. The prepared themselves for sleep, and lay down thankfully. "There will be time enough to go to Herod tomorrow, to tell him where the new-born baby lives," they said to one another.

They fell asleep. But in the night God sent each of them the same dream. In it he told them not to return to Herod, but to go home another way.

When they awoke in the morning each of the wise men told his dream to the others.

"God told me not to go back to Herod," said one.

"I too was warned," said another.

"We will depart from here and return home another way," said the third. "We will not go near Jerusalem in case the king's soldiers capture us."

So they went back to their land, and did not return to tell Herod about the baby Jesus.

After the wise men had left Mary and the

baby, and Mary had put away the gifts, they went to bed and slept.

Joseph slept soundly, but soon he dreamed a curious dream.

In his dream an angel stood by his side, just as one had done before, when he had been told Mary's secret. The angel's face was grave.

Joseph looked up at him and waited for him to speak. What a strange message the angel had brought to him!

"Arise!" he said. "Take the young child and his mother, and flee into Egypt, and stay there until I tell you to return; for Herod will seek the young child to destroy him."

Then the angel went. Joseph awoke and sat up, amazed and half afraid. He had had a strange dream, and he must tell it to Mary.

So he awoke her and told her how the angel had come to him in a dream. "And he said that we must go at once to Egypt," said Joseph. "Herod will kill Jesus if we stay here."

It was true that Herod planned to kill the little baby. He was waiting for the wise men to come back and tell him where the child was.

But they did not come. Herod waited for them impatiently, and then sent his servants to Bethlehem to find out what had happened to them.

"O King, the wise men have returned to their own country," said the servants when they came back.

"Then send after them and capture them!" cried Herod, in a fury. "They must tell me where this new-born king can be found."

But the wise men had gone too far to be captured. How then could Herod find the baby?

"I do not know if the child is one week old or one year," he said, angrily. "How can I tell? The wise men did not say how old he was."

Herod was a wicked man. He thought of a plan to kill the little Jesus, and he sent for the captain of his soldiers.

He gave him a cruel and terrible order. "Go to the city of Bethlehem and kill every boy-child under two years old!" he commanded.

"Then the baby king will be destroyed too, for he will be among them. He will not escape!"

The captain saluted and went to his men. He told them what they must do. They left the palace and were soon on their way to Bethlehem.

Once more the quiet shepherds stared in amazement as they saw the soldiers jingling by, the sun flashing on their swords.

"They go to Bethlehem!" said the shepherds in wonder. "Why should Herod's soldiers go to our quiet little town?"

They soon knew, when mothers began wailing for their poor little babies. The soldiers went about seeking the boy-babies to kill them.

The poor mothers hurried them indoors, trying to hide them. They did not understand why this terrible thing was happening to the little children of Bethlehem.

The soldiers found and killed every boy-baby. Then they rode back to Herod. "We have killed every boy-child," they said. And Herod was well pleased.

"Now the little king is dead," he said. "I need no longer be afraid that he will grow up and be king instead of me."

B ut Herod was wrong. The baby Jesus was not dead. The angel had warned Joseph to flee into Egypt on the night that the wise men had come to see Mary. Joseph knew he must obey, and he had told Mary they must go that very night.

"So soon?" said Mary, in dismay, sleepy and tired.

"Yes," said Joseph. "We will go at once, Mary. God would not send this solemn warning if there were not terrible danger. Get the little child ready while I go to saddle the donkey."

So Mary woke the sleeping Jesus and wrapped him up warmly. She packed some food for the journey, and put all their belongings into a basket. She felt anxious and fearful, for it was strange to leave like this in the middle of the night, and go to a strange country far away.

At last they were ready, and they set off to the land of Egypt. Mary and the baby rode on the donkey. Down the quiet hillside they went, past the watching shepherds and their sheep.

So, when Herod's cruel soldiers came seeking for boy-babies in Bethlehem, the little Jesus was not there. He was safe in Egypt with Joseph and Mary.

And there he grew strong and tall and kind, waiting for the day to come when he might return to his own land. Only his parents knew of the angels, the shepherds and the wise men; no one else in Egypt knew that one day the little Jesus would be the greatest king the world has ever seen.